Thank you. Check also our other book

ASIN: B09RLY9CTK

Enter this ASIN in the search engine

A lovely high contrast book for baby developing his senses and creativity

© 2022 Niunio Publishing

Diversity is beautiful thing. Every person is different. Everyone is unique

It's OK that someone prefers biking more than walking

It's OK that someone would rather swim than run

Life would be boring if everyone just did the same things and looked the same

It's OK if someone has a light skin color and another person has a dark skin color

Some people have light hair and some people have dark hair

It's your turn now.
Tell me about yourself

What is your favorite thing to do?

What color are your eyes?

Why is one skin color lighter and another darker?

Why is melanin more active in some people?

It all depends on where their families come from. Families who live in sunny areas have adapted by producing more melanin to protect their skin from the sun

Our parents come from different areas

Sometimes it's warm

Sometimes it's cold

It's sunny there

Our blood, heart, lungs, bones, and everything in our body is the same

We all have a lot in common.
People love being together
and doing lots of great things

Play

Read

Talk

Laugh

It doesn't matter if someone is tall or short

It doesn't matter if someone is skinny or overweight

All people Make up

One

Great

Family

You're part of it

The world would be boring and sad if all people were the same. Prepare different crayons and color all the people

Printed in Great Britain
by Amazon